Mine for a Year

Mine for a Year

text and photographs by
Susan Kuklin

Coward–McCann, Inc.

New York

Library of Congress Cataloging in Publication Data
Kuklin, Susan.   Mine for a year.
Summary: Text and illustrations describe a foster
child's year spent socializing a puppy destined to be
trained as a dog guide for a blind person.
1. Foster home care—Juvenile literature. 2. Children
and animals—Juvenile literature. 3. Guide dogs—
Training of—Juvenile literature. [1. Foster home care.
2. Dogs. 3. Guide dogs] I. Title.
HV715.K84 1984   362.7′33   83-23916
ISBN 0-698-20603-7

For Bailey, with love

Acknowledgments

I would like to thank the following people and organizations who helped make this book possible:

John Dumshat at the 4-H Extension Services, Warren County, N.J.; the families and friends who participated in "Puppy Power" 4-H Club, Hackettstown, N.J.; Dr. David M. Inkeles at the Eye Physicians of Sussex County, N.J.; Dr. Alexander Cojocar at the Hackettstown, N.J. Animal Hospital; Camp Marcella and the New Jersey Commission for the Blind, David Barhart, director; Allamuchy School, Allamuchy, N.J.; and Hackettstown Middle School, Hackettstown, N.J.

I would also like to thank the following friends for their help and encouragement during my year with George and Doug: Gregory and Jane Vitiello, Susan and Allan Bloom, Carolyn Trager

My understanding editor, Refna Wilkin, always was available to give me invaluable encouragement and advice. Nanette Stevenson, my art director, paid great personal attention to the design of the book. I am especially grateful to my agent Jane Wilson at JCA Literary Agency, who was always full of cheer, spirit and perseverance.

Lastly, I'd like to express my appreciation to Evelyn Henderson who so graciously opened her home and her family to me and my camera. Knowing her has enriched my life. Thanks Ev.

When Evelyn Henderson's parents died a number of years ago she was left alone in a large farmhouse. She wanted to do something—something that would help other people. She sold the farm and bought a smaller one. Then she met with a social worker to see if she could be a foster mother to young girls. Although there were no girls, two brothers were in need of a foster home. Evelyn provided that home. Since that time a total of twenty-six foster boys have lived with Ev.

Evelyn arranged for each of her boys to join her local 4-H club. For years she has been a member of Puppy Power: a 4-H project that places eight-to-twelve-week-old puppies with families for one year before they are trained to be dog guides for blind persons. Here is a program that is lots of fun and also teaches some basic lessons about giving to others.

The puppy project would not only give her boys a sense of purpose but teach them to be responsible as well. The boys, some of whom have had little chance to be close to another person, would have the opportunity to relate to cuddly, loving puppies which would return their affection. Ev also thought that by going through the process of loving a puppy and then giving it up, her boys would have a positive experience of losing something they loved to counterbalance some of the negative experiences of loss they might previously have had. Losses aren't all bad. Sometimes they are important parts of growing up.

Evelyn and her boys have raised over two hundred puppies. This is the story of George, one of her boys, and his first pup, Doug, told as George sees it.

Mine for a Year

That's my brother, Paul, racing to the 4-H van in front of me. "Oh, wow . . . lookit here . . . WOW!" he cried as we first saw my puppy.

"Come to me . . . here, Dougie . . . here, boy," I said. "You're mine, Dougie . . . my very first pup! LOOK! He likes me! He likes me!"

I showed Doug to my brothers.

"He's neat, George," Jimmy said. "Can I hold him?"

"This is Jimmy, Doug, and this is my natural brother, Paul. They already have puppies. Now we all do!"

When I put Doug down and started toward the house, he tried to follow me but he fell over his overgrown, floppy paws.

"This is our foster mother, Ev, Doug. And that's Itsy. He's our family dog. He can be mean, so watch out for him. Ev says he's a Napoleon because he's smaller than the other dogs."

Eight weeks ago the 4-H representative had called to tell me that a puppy named Doug had just been born. Now it was May and he was here. A black labrador retriever—just what I wanted.

I carried Doug all around the farm and introduced him to his new home and all the other animals who live there.

"These are my brothers' pups. You have to learn to get along with lots of people and other animals. You're not just some ordinary dog. You're special. You're going to become a dog guide some day."

Then Evelyn called us. "You better bring Doug into the house and feed him. It's getting late."

I brought Doug into the kitchen and showed him his food bowl. Doug had been eating with his littermates in the kennel. Now suddenly he found himself in a strange home where he had his own dish and nobody was fighting for food. I had learned from training sessions at my 4-H club that it was important for dog guides not to become fussy eaters. A blind person wouldn't want to sit around all day waiting for a dog to eat.

I sat down on the floor beside Doug to keep his attention on the dish until he finished eating. "I'm supposed to feed you three times a day when you're little." Doug sniffed his dish. "You'll eat just before me so that you won't beg at the table. Then you'll have manners, Doug. You'll learn to sit under the table when I eat just as you will when you're older and work with a blind person."

After dinner we went outside to play. I gave him some ice cubes to chew. Puppies love ice cubes, especially when they are teething. Once it became dark, we played inside the house. I told him that we were going to be best friends for a whole year. "After that you'll have to go back to the kennel, where you'll be trained to be a dog guide. Don't worry, a year's a long time from now. I'm going to make you the best dog guide candidate in the whole world. Someone your future blind master will be proud of. I'll be proud of you, too, Doug. Someday I might need a dog just like you 'cause someday I may be blind too."

I often worried about my vision. I'd had three operations on my eyes already. None of them made me see much better. I still needed to wear thick glasses. No one knew yet whether my eyes were going to get better or stay the same or get worse.

For Doug's first night away from his littermates, I put him in his crate in the living room. Doug just cried and cried so I carried him downstairs to my room. The puppies are not supposed to sleep in bed with us kids because often an older blind person does not like sleeping with a dog. It's not fair to the blind person who is trying to establish a relationship if he has to begin by retraining the dog.

I pulled my sleeping bag from the closet and slept on the floor with Doug. I sang to him and told him stories. I sang the songs that I sang at Spring Music Festival.

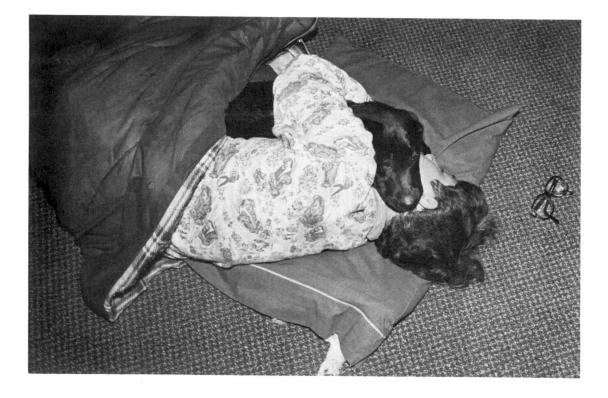

Thursday evening, after supper, we all go to 4-H club meeting. That's where the dogs have obedience training. I'd been to class before and even took part in the exercises with my brothers' dogs. Now Ev thought I was old enough and well enough to have a puppy all my own.

This night I ate real fast and helped Ev do the dishes without her even having to ask. "What's the hurry, George?" she asked. I think she was laughing.

"It's Doug's first 4-H meeting. Wait till everybody sees my new puppy!"

The meeting was held in front of the firehouse. Everyone liked Doug. Mrs. Lund, my fifth grade teacher, whose daughter, Kristen, is in the club, said Doug was adorable. She asked if he was a barker.

"No," I told her, "he's perfect."

My first job was to teach Doug to walk with a loose leash. Doug was supposed to walk briskly at my left side. Dog guides are trained always to walk on their master's left. In this way the blind person can hold the dog's harness with the left hand and the right hand is free. We walked in a circle with the other kids and their dogs. The dogs must learn not to become distracted by one another. Later that could mean a great deal to the blind person whose safety depends on the dog.

"You have your work cut out for you, George!" shouted Mr. Bauer, the club's leader. "Remember," he instructed us as we worked our dogs, "when you teach obedience, see that your dog comes to your left side first. Call him by name. Give him lots of love. Lots of praise. Scratch him behind the ears. If your puppy goes away, give him a little tug and then a loose leash. It should be a happy event for him to come to you."

During my first day at obedience training with Doug I didn't say much. I just walked my dog and gave him a few tugs on the leash. The other dogs looked so much bigger. I wasn't sure about how Doug would react. I didn't want to embarrass my new puppy. Or me.

The leader saw me struggling with the new lessons and came over to work with us. He said, "George, first call your dog by name and then say 'down.' If he won't lie, gently take his front legs and ease him down. If then he doesn't want to get up, give him a little jerk on his collar. That will do it. Do the exercise a few times and then play. We don't want him to get bored. Later, do it again."

At the end of the training session we gathered around as the leader explained some of the fine points of training a puppy. "If you call your dog and then smack him, he won't come to you again. Never hit him. Your dog will respond to the tone of your voice. He wants to please you."

After school each day we would practice. Although Doug was unaware of it, I knew that come summer it would be time for the county fair. For years I'd dreamed of winning a blue ribbon just like the one that hung in Floyd's room. (Floyd is Ev's oldest foster son.) The blue ribbon is for best in obedience. To win one is a big deal. I really wanted Doug to win.

"Doug, sit," I said and gently pushed down on his rear the

way the leader taught me. "Doug, up," I commanded and I slapped my thigh as a signal to rise while I pulled up on the leash. When Doug did not respond I said, "Oh shame, Doug," in a deep mournful tone. Doug wanted desperately to please me. His ears went down and his tail tucked under. "That's all right, boy. I know it takes a long time to learn all this." I hugged my dog.

I tried another approach. I made a hand signal in front of Doug's face and said, "Doug, stay." By placing my hand in front of my dog's vision, he stayed still. Then I walked back, still holding the leash, and said, "Doug, come." When Doug came I gave him tons of praise. "You're a great Dougie . . . such a wonderful fella . . . I love ya . . ."

In June I brought Doug to school for "Show and Tell." At first I was very nervous standing in front of the entire class with my dog. I don't like to speak in class. It embarrasses me. Then I began telling about my project and all the things I must do to raise Doug to become a dog guide. Soon I forgot my nervousness. "This is Doug. He's mine for a year. I have to give him a lot of love and attention so that he will be used to people and love them. I have to teach him manners and I have to teach him to obey rules."

"That's called socializing a puppy," our teacher explained to my classmates.

24

"Doug needs to learn that since he will become a dog guide and take a blind person all around. He'll be allowed to go places that other dogs and pets can't go. To stores and restaurants and on buses and airplanes. He'll be taught to watch out for traffic when crossing the street with his master and to look for danger like holes in the sidewalk."

"Do you teach him all that, George?" one of the kids asked.

"No, a professional trainer does it after my year with him. It's my job to make Doug a well-rounded dog. The trainers have a saying that dog guides must love to learn and learn to love. My job's really to love him a lot."

"He's a really neat dog, George," said Charlie. The kids kept coming closer and closer.

"Yeah, I know, a great dog," I said. Doug enjoyed all the attention. He sat quietly the whole time and looked curiously at all the kids.

"I wish my mother would let me have a dog like that. How can I get one?"

"First you have to be a member of 4-H. Then you have to prove that you are responsible enough to take care of a dog like this. Your mother can tell the 4-H leader if she thinks you can do it. Then you have to wait for a litter to be born."

"When's that?"

"When the trainer sees a particularly smart and healthy dog, the dog is sent to the stud farm and mated. The puppies are named by computer. The computer was up to 'D' when Doug was born so that's how he got his name. Each dog has a number tattooed in his ear to identify him as a dog guide."

All the kids gathered even closer. Each one wanted to pet Doug or give him a little hug. Doug didn't mind at all.

"Is he housebroken?"

"Well . . . sorta," I said. I didn't want to embarrass Doug but I remembered his accident late last night. I heard him begin to piddle. I jumped out of bed and dragged him to the yard. Doug left a trail through the living room. It was a mess.

"How do you housebreak him?" Sarah pressed me. "I could never have a dog unless he was housebroken."

"Every day I take him to the same spot for him to go to the bathroom. The trainers call it 'emptying.' Then at night I put a short leash on him and tie him to the front of my bed. He won't empty where he sleeps, so if he wants to go, he'll make a racket and wake me up. I jump up and rush him outside to the spot where he's supposed to go. The short leash also trains him to stay beside the master's bed in case the blind person needs him in the middle of the night."

"What happens when it rains?" practical Melinda asked.

"I get wet," I said.

"Oooooh, he's so cute and friendly. How can you give up such a wonderful pet?"

"Doug is not a pet," I said firmly. "He's a working dog. Anyway, I don't have to give him up for a whole year. A year's a long time from now."

"He's a nice dog, George. You must be very special to have a dog like that," Rachel said admiringly.

"I am," I said. Doug rewarded my talk with a big, slurpy kiss.

Once school was out for the summer, Doug went everywhere with me, even to get glasses. I hadn't wanted to talk about it, but finally I told Evelyn of the headaches I was having almost every day.

"It doesn't mean you're losing your sight, George. It could be because you're growing. Your glasses are pressing into your temples," Evelyn said. "Let's see what larger frames will do."

I took Doug with me for moral support. Ev was right. My headaches went away once I had the new glasses.

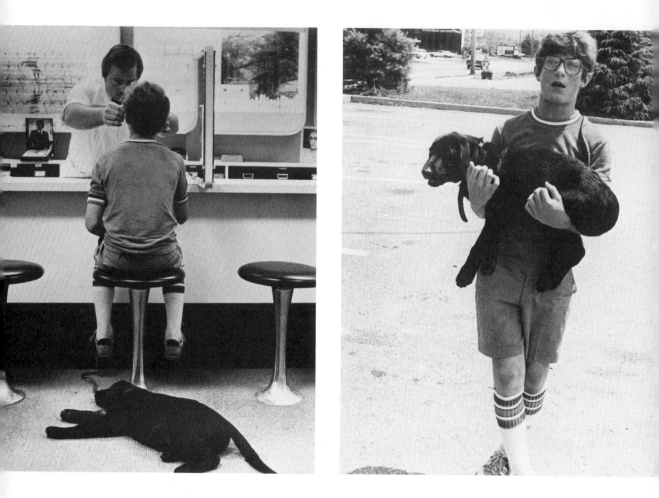

It was hot when we came out of the optician's office and I worried about Doug burning his paws on the asphalt. I picked him up and carried him to Ev's van. "See, Doug, I'll take care of you now and later you'll take care of me, right?"

Doug liked it when I carried him places. In fact, I was learning that Doug's two favorite activities were being carried and sleeping. A puppy needs lots of sleep.

30

"Ev . . . Ev . . . Doug's fainted!" I called as I ran into the house one day.

"What?" screamed Ev. She dropped the pot she was drying and came running to meet me.

"Look, Ev, I told Doug it was time for obedience training and he just keeled over on his back with his big paws up. He *fainted*."

"He fainted, huh? You'd better watch it, George. You're spoiling that dog. Spoiled dogs do not make good dog guides."

When Doug made up his mind not to do something, he would just lie down. I called it "fainting." Ev called it something else.

"Dougie, Ev says you are bullheaded. You better shape up," I said to Doug. Doug was not impressed. "You know something else, Doug? You're getting heavy."

Paul brought his dog, Glider, with Ev and me when I took Doug to the vet. The doctor listened to Doug's heart and lungs to make sure they were all right. Then he checked his teeth. "He's losing some of his baby teeth, George, and his perfect teeth are coming in just right. They are nice and white. He has an excellent bite."

When the doctor checked his ears he found some wax and signs of ear mites. He took a swab with alcohol and cleaned them out. Then he put some medicine into each ear to kill the mites. He told me to swab Doug's ears carefully every day for six weeks and then the mites would be gone.

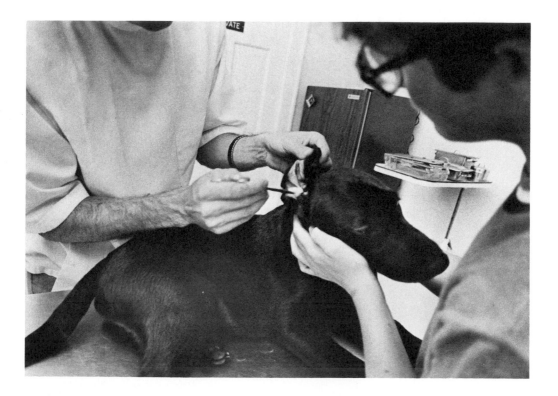

"Hang on to your dog for me," the doctor said as he was about to give Doug his vaccination. Sometimes a pup will try to nip the vet when he gives him a shot in his rear. I knew Doug would never do that, but I held his face in my hands and talked to him just in case he became frightened. Doug didn't feel a thing.

"I can see that Doug's getting a lot of good care," the doctor said. "Just keep an eye out for mites." I shook hands with the doctor and thanked him. Doug thanked him, too, in his own special way.

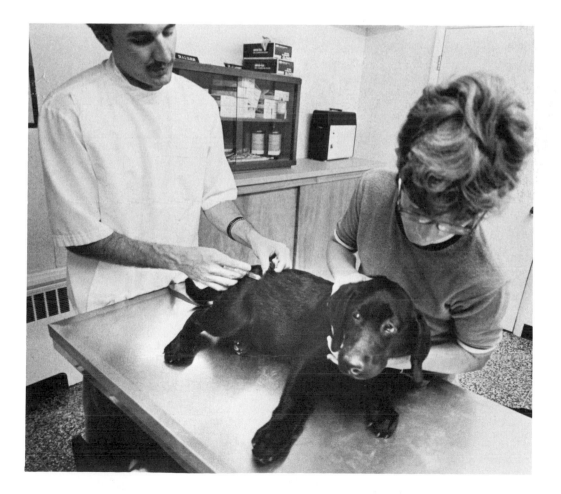

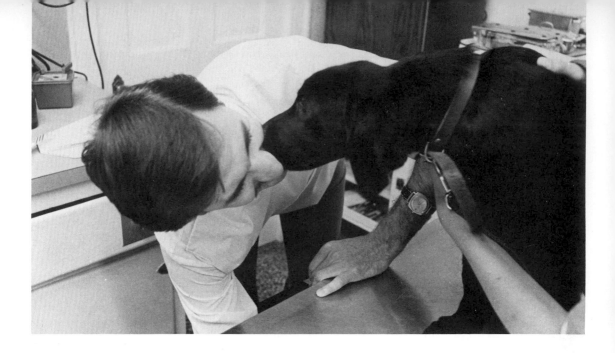

Each day Doug and I would go off together and talk. I told him everything about myself. It was easy for me to share my fears about my eyes with him. I tried to hide these feelings from my brother Paul because I didn't want my kid brother to worry about me. Ev worried about me too. But Doug was something else. Doug would listen to me for hours and not ask stupid questions or cry or anything like that. He would just give me one of his big slurpy kisses and then run off to play.

In the mornings he would lumber after me as I did my chores. We collected tomatoes from the garden and eggs from the henhouse. When we were feeding the goats Doug was warned, "Watch it! Our goat Deuxième butts!"

Doug learned his lessons well: Stay close to me when collecting tomatoes and eggs, keep away from Deuxième, and faint when Ev asks us to weed the garden.

34

The day before the county fair there was lots of excitement in our house. First Jimmy brushed his dog, Chief, and then Paul took the brush to spruce up Glider. I checked Doug for ticks and fleas. I brushed his coat till it was smooth and shiny. Doug thought grooming time was playtime.

"Come on, Doug, be serious. You have to look good when you win the blue ribbon," I said. I was worried. There was lots of pressure on me. In a few weeks I was due for an eye examination and that was always a tense time. And now there was this blue ribbon competition. Doug hadn't had that much obedience training as yet.

"Awwwwww, you're not going to win. Chief and I will win," said Jimmy as he blew down the house of cards he was building.

"I will too win. Doug knows how much I want to win, don't you, Dougie?"

"How can any of us win with Craig and his dog, Dwyer, in the competition?" Paul asked, stepping between us just in case things got out of hand.

"Doug can beat Dwyer," I said.

"But nobody can beat Craig," my brother said. "He's not president of the club for nothing. And Craig's been working with his dog for almost a year now. Doug is too little."

"My Doug can beat anybody, can't you, Dougie?" I brushed him even harder.

The day of the fair was unusually rainy and cold for the middle of July. I put on layers of T-shirts in the hope of peeling them off once the sun came out. A few of Evelyn's older foster boys returned to the farm to pack sandwiches and help Ev with the younger kids and their dogs. Everyone piled into Ev's van. Off we went singing and laughing in the high hopes of returning with at least one blue ribbon.

I was pretty quiet though. Ev couldn't tell whether I was nervous about the competition or about my doctor's appointment. She kept asking me but I just didn't want to talk about it. Doug knew all about it but he wasn't talking either.

At the fairground I carefully carried Doug so that he wouldn't get his paws full of mud. As I checked into the 4-H tent I saw the other members of my club all gathered around Craig.

"Hiya, George . . . how's your dog?" Craig asked. He looked like a winner already.

"Fine," I said and moved a little behind Ev. "I'm gonna take Doug to see the other exhibits, Ev."

"OK, George, but don't be too long and keep Doug clean," she called as we disappeared.

Away from the tent and the other kids I felt more relaxed. I almost forgot about winning the blue ribbon as we visited the livestock exhibits and the amusements. Doug liked the sounds and smells at the fair. I was proud when people came up to me and asked me about my dog. One of the farmers shook my hand and said, "That's a fine thing you're doing, young fella . . . raising your dog to go out and help some blind person somewhere. Real fine." I had almost forgotten

that this was the real reason for having Doug: to help another person, not win blue ribbons. But one thing at a time. Doug could become a dog guide later but now he had to win a blue ribbon.

As the competition began I lined up with the other kids and their dogs. At first we put our dogs through obedience training as a group to warm up the animals and feel more comfortable performing in front of an audience. Each member of 4-H was called by name to work his dog. I was

nervous. Doug was sleepy. "Don't faint on me today, Doug, whatever you do."

"George and his dog, Doug, please," the judge announced.

"Oh no, I'm gonna be sick," I thought.

"George . . ." the judge called again.

Carefully I placed a choker collar around Doug's neck. This would give me more control. A swift yank gets the dog's attention. It's the sound of the snap that does it. The dogs have such large necks and so much skin that it doesn't hurt at all.

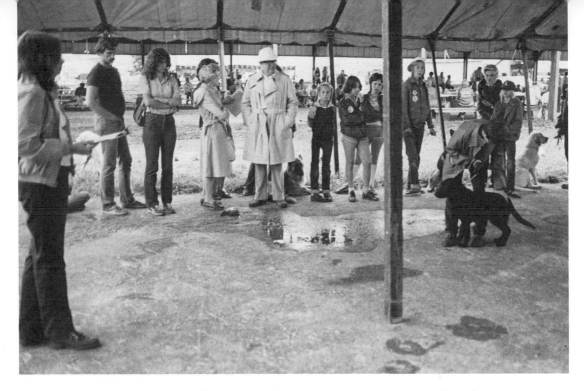

"Doug, sit," I began. I heard my voice crack. My hand wouldn't stop shaking. "Doug, down . . . good boy . . . Doug, stay." Doug listened to my commands and obeyed me.

"And now we'll test the figure eight," the judge announced. This exercise is to test how well the dog responds to his master and avoids the other animals. "Can I have two club members with their dogs stand at either end of the rink?"

Two kids stepped forward. They knew the judges would be watching them, too. Not only did the judges look at how well the walking dog performed, but they watched whether the sitting dogs ignored the approaching dogs as well.

"Come on, Doug . . . good boy . . ." I said. I could see that Doug was becoming tired.

"Praise your dog, George, give him lots of praise," a 4-H leader called.

"I can't hear you!" one of the kids in my club yelled.

I wished my friends in the audience would shut up. I tried not to let the judge see me tug at the leash. Doug wanted to keep up but I was moving faster than usual. "Come on, boy. Just one more loop around. That's a good boy. A little more."

At last it was over. All in all I thought we did a pretty good job. I went running toward Ev. "How'd it look? How'd it look?"

"Pretty good, George. I was proud of both of you," she said. I had so many questions about my performance but I heard Craig begin to work his dog. "Dwyer, sit; Dwyer, down; Dwyer, stay, atta boy, great fella . . . now Dwyer, come . . ." Hearing Craig give crisp, confident commands, I turned to watch. My dream of a blue ribbon was quickly disappearing. "He's really great," I said softly to no one in particular. "Just like a pro." I rested my hand on top of Doug's head so he wouldn't be too disappointed. Everyone cheered as Craig finished a masterful performance.

Doug and I moved off alone to an empty bleacher while the judges huddled together. Then I took a deep breath and walked up to Craig. "You were great, Craig," I said.

"Thanks, George," he replied. "You weren't so bad yourself. You've got a real nice dog there."

The judges marched to the center of the rink. "Everyone was so wonderful that we decided that each one of you will receive an honorable mention ribbon. We are very proud to announce that this year's blue ribbon goes to Craig and his dog, Dwyer."

Once the fair was over, I spent all my time teaching Doug. Sitting under the flowering quince in the late afternoon, I told Doug what it would be like to be a dog guide. "When you wear a harness you will be working, leading your master all around. You will be able to go everywhere with your master. When you're not wearing your harness, you'll be able to play just like you do here. It'll be a nice life for you, you'll see."

During the summer the 4-H club did many activities together. We went swimming and to picnics in the national park. We took our puppies to old age homes so the elderly people could play with the dogs. We kids sang them camp songs and told them all about our project.

We even spent a Sunday afternoon at Camp Marcella. This camp was set up especially to meet the needs of blind children. The campers were very interested in our project. Some of them sat with Doug and me and talked about the Special Olympics that they took part in. I wanted to hear about all their activities—especially sports. Next to reading, sports was the one thing I didn't want to give up if I became blind. I was relieved to hear I wouldn't have to.

The campers, on the other hand, wanted to know about Doug. One teenager told me that when she became eighteen, the earliest a person can have a dog guide, she hoped it would be Doug.

"Well, only if I can't have him," I said.

"I can't play with you today, Doug. I have to go to the eye doctor. Ev says you have to stay here." I brushed him like I did each morning and gave him his vitamin pill. Once more I told him about my eye problem just to be sure he understood. Doug listened very carefully. "The doctor told me I have cataracts. That's when the lens in the eye gets all cloudy so you can't see anymore. He said we all have a lens in the back of each eye, behind our pupil. We don't see them but they are there. You have them, too, Doug. When we get older they can become cloudy and the doctors don't know how to clean them up. So they take them out. That's what they did to me. They took out the lenses from the back of my eyes and gave me cataract glasses. The doctor told me that cataracts are common in older people but it is not usual when you are young like me. If you live to be ninety, Doug, you might have cataracts."

I didn't like leaving Doug behind. I was scared that I'd
have to have another operation. I gave Doug an extra-hard
hug. "You know what I'm gonna do?" I whispered in his
ear. "No matter what the doctor says, I'm going to tell him I
can see fine. No more operations. After all, if I'm sick in the
hospital how can I play with you? Remember, this is our
secret. Don't even tell Ev."

Evelyn and I weren't there long before the doctor came to the door of the waiting room.

"Here's my prize patient. How are you today, George?"

"Fine," I said, remembering my vow to Doug.

"How are the glasses?"

"Fine," I said. The doctor could hardly hear me, I spoke so low. I hated to lie, but after all, I'd made a promise to Doug.

"Come in and let's have a look." I marched in while looking to Ev to follow me. I didn't want to go through this alone. The doctor was nice and friendly but I was worried. Ev closed the door and took a seat facing me, out of the way of the doctor and his equipment.

"Last year when you had surgery, and I took the lenses from your eyes, I also had to take out a liquid called 'vitreous.' Because of this, the glasses prescription changes. That's why I must keep checking. It is important that you tell me how your eyes feel so that I can be sure you have the proper glasses. First I'm going to use this blue light to check the pressure in your eyes. It won't hurt. I've done this before." The doctor worked quickly as he spoke to me.

"How's that?"

"Fine," I said. I wasn't really sure whether or not it was fine.

"Is this better, or this?" The doctor began trying different lenses.

"Fine," I said.

"What's fine? Why do you keep saying 'fine'? You've got to level with me, George." The doctor continued to switch lenses. I was embarrassed.

48

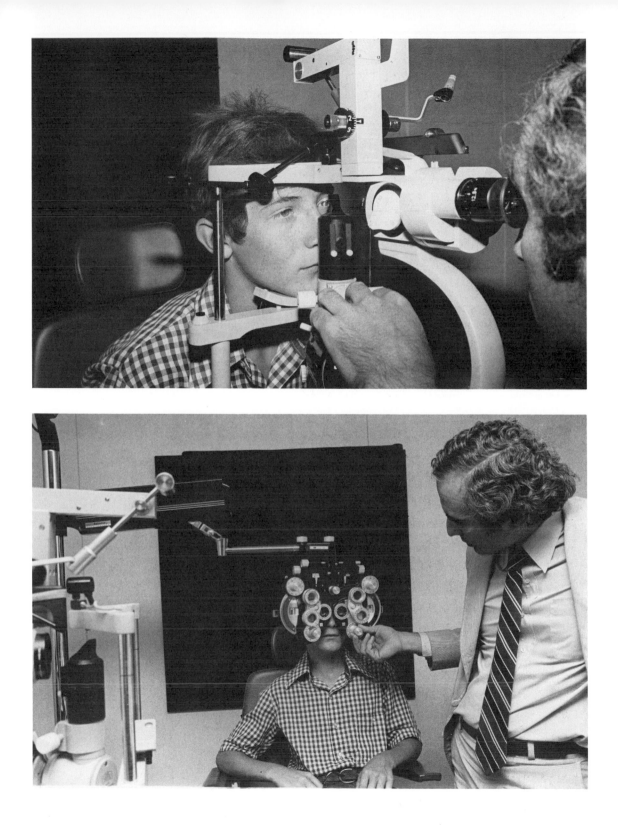

"Oh, oh, this one is better . . . *much* better!" I yelled. It really was better. Everything looked sharper than ever before. The muscles around my eyes relaxed as I looked around.

Soon the doctor said, "All right. That's it. From now on when you come for a checkup I'll just examine your glasses. Chances are you won't need another operation."

"Really? For real?" I could hardly believe it.

"For real," the doctor laughed. "You don't have to say 'fine' anymore. You're my favorite success."

My eyes filled with tears. Everything was blurry, but this time when I wiped my eyes, all was clear again.

"Now you're not going to see as well with your left eye as with your right eye. It just never was as good and it never will be. But it will be even better than it is now. OK. Be well."

I was speechless. I wanted to thank the doctor. I wanted to tell him how grateful I was but the words just weren't there. With that one sentence—"chances are you won't need another operation"—my life changed. No longer would I have to worry about becoming blind.

"Ev, Ev, did you hear that? I'm gonna be all right. The doctor said it. NO MORE OPERATIONS!"

"Oh, George, that's the best news," cried Ev, tears streaming down her face. She gave me the biggest hug.

"Let's go home and tell Doug." I was out of the doctor's building and into the car in a flash. "Poor Doug, he's been so worried."

"Doug! Doug! Dougie! I'm not going to be blind after all!" Doug raced toward me with his ears flopping up and down. "Yahooo . . . no more operations! Look at me, Dougie, I can see . . ." I danced and pranced all over the lawn. Doug wanted to join in but I frightened him. He would rush up to me and then hightail it away from such silly goings-on. I just couldn't stop. I ran and laughed and turned cartwheels all over the place. At last we collapsed. I tried to carry him back to the house. "I love ya, Dougie, I really do, boy, but you're getting too heavy."

As the seasons changed and fall turned to winter, Doug and I continued to work and play. I was in middle school now and had more homework than last year when I was in grade school. Doug was growing bigger and stronger. Now he looked just as big as Paul and Jimmy's dogs. I was growing too. I felt more comfortable with other people.

Doug would lie beside me as I did my homework, just as one day he would lie beside his blind master, ready in case the blind person needed his help.

The chores of running a farm and keeping large dogs did not let up once the cold weather arrived. I hated having to go out and clean the "emptying" yard. Doug and the other dogs didn't seem to mind the cold weather. They had warm coats. Having Doug was fun but there was also a lot of hard work.

At 4-H meetings Doug proved to be an excellent example for the newer dogs. He rarely tugged at his leash and he ignored the other dogs when lining up and going through the sit-down-stay-come exercises. During one of the meet-

ings all the kids put on blindfolds and went through a series of experiments to understand what it felt like to be blind. Before my visit to the doctor, I hated exercises like this one, but now I was interested. At first I trained Doug with the idea that someday I would be repaid for my effort when I needed a dog guide. Now things had changed. I trained

Doug so that I would help someone in need. I didn't care about being paid back. My love for Doug and his devotion in return were enough.

But I was still curious about how it was to be blind. I tried to pour juice into a glass. I put my index finger into the glass so that I could feel it when the liquid reached the top. Ev watched from behind. She was so grateful that I would no longer have to worry about such things.

In March it was my thirteenth birthday. "I'm a teenager now, Doug, you better treat me with respect," I told him. Ev gave me a party. The kids from the 4-H club were invited, and so were many from my class. Doug was the only dog. The others were put in the yard during the party. Doug was used to having lots of people around and he especially liked little kids.

By early spring, Doug was full grown. Although I was not full grown, I was changing too. Each morning I checked my face for whiskers. There were none as yet but I knew they were coming. Evelyn bought me special soap because she said my skin was becoming more oily. I didn't much care about that.

"But Elizabeth will care . . ." Jimmy teased. I never should have told him about my new girlfriend.

"You shut up, Jimmy!" I stomped into my room and slammed the door. More and more I needed to be alone—alone with Doug, of course. I moved Doug's feeding bowl into my room and stayed with him there while he ate.

The 4-H activities became even more complicated. One Saturday we all met in the parking lot behind Bach's drugstore to take our dogs for a walk through town. The 4-H leaders wanted us to be sure the dogs were well-behaved and under control in towns and on busy streets. It was important that they not be distracted by traffic or by one another.

"Control your dogs! Control your dogs!" Mrs. Kassay shouted. "As soon as you get their attention, praise them. Keep them interested."

It's really important that a dog who's to become a dog guide is self-assured and not frightened by traffic or stores. The blind person must have complete confidence in the dog.

One by one each 4-Her took a dog into the bank, the hardware store, the post office, and the drugstore. "Nice job you're doing," the chemist called to me.

"Thanks, Mr. Joseph," I replied.

After the walk the kids rested their dogs and then watered them. Both Paul and Jimmy's dogs had gone back to the kennel. Now they had new puppies to train. I was beginning to think of the new pup I would get after Doug.

"When does Doug leave you to go to be trained?" Sabrina asked.

"Right after Puppy Camp. Ev said she'd ask if he could stay with me at least until then."

"Are you getting another dog?"

"Yep, a black lab, just like Doug," I said as I hugged him.

Puppy Camp is where children who raise dog guides gather together with their puppies for a weekend of activities. This year it was held at Beemersville, a 4-H farm in New Jersey. Kids came from three states. Usually a parent goes along to help with meals and keep an eye on us kids. Ev had gone in the past and this was the first time she couldn't go. There was a good chance we boys wouldn't be allowed to go at all.

"Please, please, Ev. I'll watch Paul and Jimmy. I'm old enough," I begged her. I knew if we didn't go to the camp, Doug would never, ever have that opportunity again.

"Will you promise to mind the dogs and not run off and leave them with some parent?" Ev said.

"We promise . . . we promise," the three of us sang and we each checked each other to be sure no one was crossing his fingers.

Ev was a pushover when we really wanted something. She thought each of us who came to live in her house was special. Although we knew that she would never back down when the rules of the house were at stake, she usually let us have what we wanted—if she could afford it. Anyway, we were pretty good kids. She worked hard to get us that way.

At camp the dogs stayed under the table while all the kids ate, just as they would later at the training camp with their future masters. The campers were broken up into four groups. I was in the blue group. Paul and Jimmy were in others. We played Frisbee-soccer and went on a scavenger hunt.

All the groups gathered under trees to hear more about training our dogs. Counselors checked the dogs for ear mites and ticks. I later took home a bottle of vinegar and water so that I could carefully wash Doug's ears before he went off to the training kennel.

In the afternoon, Doug and I and Paul and his new puppy, Lincoln, explored the woods. Doug didn't tire as much as he did when he was little. But he did get very hot. I tried to wet him down with the hose but I had trouble doing it. So we went into our bunk and got into the shower, clothes and all.

I wanted Doug to have a good time. I knew this was the last adventure we would have together. I tried not to think about it, but actually I couldn't think of anything else.

The morning Doug was to be returned to the kennel, I didn't feel too well. Most of the night was spent in the bathroom. Evelyn tried to give me some tea and toast but I couldn't keep anything down. I told Evelyn I was taking Doug into the yard for one more obedience session, "just to make sure he does everything right." Actually I wanted to be alone with Doug. Ev understood. She'd been through this many times before.

"You're going to school today, Doug," I said, taking his head in my hands. "Today, you go off to a great adventure. You will go to the kennel and you'll play with other dogs. Then you'll be assigned to a trainer who will work with you a half hour every day for three months. He'll play with you, give you lots of love. Then you'll meet your new master, the blind person who you will live with and guide for the rest of your life. Your new master will be with you twenty-four hours a day. You won't have to wait around as you did for me to come home from school. You're going to have a great life and make me proud of you. It's a funny thing—I'll never know your new master. I won't know whether it's a man or a woman or anything. And that person will never know me. The trainers explained that it's important that your new master become your very best friend and to do that you must forget about me. You'll never see me again. That makes me so sad. But it'll be OK because I'll know that you're out there somewhere in the world helping someone. It's nice to know that I've done something special for someone. It makes me feel special, just like you. You're the bond between the two of us. Thank you for giving that to me, Doug. Oh, Dougie . . . a year's not such a long time after all . . ."

Doug and I stayed under the trees all curled up in each other's arms for the longest time. As the 4-H van pulled into the driveway, the other boys rushed to the car. "Where's the new puppy? Can we see him?" the boys asked as the 4-H representative climbed from the driver's seat.

"He's hiding," she replied and waved to me to bring Doug into the house.

I sat with the representative at the kitchen table and filled out forms about Doug's personality and training. This information would be of help to Doug's new trainer. I told her how good he was. He was relaxed in the car and loved to go places. He rarely barked and he was a pretty good eater.

"Don't forget that he faints, George," Paul added, thinking he was being a big help.

I stared at Paul crosseyed. The only thing I wanted to play down were the so-called fainting episodes. After all, a dog who faints, even one who's faking it, does not make a good dog guide.

68

"When does he faint, George?" the representative asked me. She was smiling but I didn't want to take any chances.

"Oh, only when he doesn't want to do something," Jimmy added happily.

"Will you all shut up and let me handle this," I said. I was ready to strangle them. They just sat there with big, Cheshire cat grins smeared across their faces.

"That's all right, George. I can see Doug is a wonderful dog. Whoever gets him will forever be grateful to you. You should be very proud," the representative said.

"I am," I said, fighting back the tears. "Doug's a great dog."

Quietly, without being asked, I took Doug outside. I tenderly lifted Doug's collar and together we walked into the

4-H van. "Be a good boy, Dougie, make me proud of you. I love ya, fella." After a few last kisses and a hug, I closed the van. As the van pulled out of the driveway, we all ran after it shouting goodbye to Doug.

Jimmy and Paul put their arms around my shoulders as we returned up the hill. Each of them had been through this before and knew how I felt.

At the top of the hill, Ev put her arms around me and said softly, "There's someone waiting for you, George."

"My new puppy?" I asked. I was exhausted, too numb to cry or feel anything. All I wanted was to forget the last hour, to turn back the clock and be with my friend again. Ev led me to the back of her van.

"This is Yuri, your new puppy."

"Hi, Yuri. Here, boy," I managed to say. "Oh, Ev, he looks just like Doug looked that first day. Yuri? Yuri? Here, fella."

Yuri scampered out of the crate and into my arms, sniffed me cautiously and began to lick my face.

"LOOK!" I shouted. "He likes me! He likes me!"

I put the puppy on the grass and began to run backward. "Here, boy, here, Yuri." Yuri flopped after me, falling over his own feet. "Look! He knows me already! Come on, Yuri . . . atta boy . . . come on . . . we have a whole year together . . . a year is an awfully long time . . . we'll have lots of adventures . . . ."

George did see Doug once more. Three months after Doug left the Henderson farm he completed training as a dog guide. Before Doug was assigned a new master, the trainer invited George to watch him go through his paces. George had to stand a short distance away so that Doug wouldn't see him. Doug put on a world-class performance. He looked wonderful in his harness, self-assured and happy. George was very proud.